BORDER LANDS

SHROPSHIRE & THE WELSH MARCHES

JULIAN CRITCHLEY & DAVID PATERSON

❦

First published in Great Britain by:
PEAK PUBLISHING LTD
88 Cavendish Road
London SW12 0DF.

❦

ISBN 0 9521908 0 X

❦

❦

British Library Cataloguing in Publication Data applied for.

❦

Paterson, David
Borderlands. Shropshire and the Marches.
1. Shropshire and Herefordshire.
I. Title. II. Critchley, Julian

❦

Designed by Jim Downie.
Typeset in Bembo Roman 12/16 by Department S.
Edited by Morrison Halcrow.
Originated and printed by Toppan Co. (S) PTe.

CONTENTS

THE LONGMYND

BLUE

REMEMBERED

HILLS

CLUN FOREST

INTRODUCTION

This book is not a gazetteer; it is not even a guide book. It is a celebration of the beauties of Shropshire and the Welsh border as seen through the eyes of a photographer, David Paterson, and my pen.

I was not born in Shropshire, although I now live in Ludlow. My mother was born in a cottage at Wistanstow in 1898, the fifth child of a family of six, the daughter of a railway worker on the old London and North Western. She became a nurse, and married a doctor. To that extent she quit South Shropshire for London and the wider world. But, in a bid to escape the Luftwaffe, I was evacuated to live with her eldest brother, Campbell Morris, and his family in the maternal cottage. I went to the village school and then to Brockhurst, Church Stretton, a preparatory school for the children of the middle class. Later, I went to Shrewsbury where I spent three and a half undistinguished years under John Wolfenden, running for my life. Shrewsbury in the '40s was much like Arnold's Rugby a century before.

I have returned frequently to Shropshire, staying with friends and relations. If I claimed to know the county "like the back of my hand", it would be false. The unfamiliar view, the village unvisited for a quarter of a century, a strange, damp-smelling church, all these are part of the delights of gentle exploration. What I will claim is a love for Shropshire and the borders. My spirits rise when I glimpse again a "blue, remembered hill", or walk through the streets of Ludlow early on a Sunday morning. Shropshire's voices are as attractive as Shropshire's dales, but impossible to reproduce in type. I have written about Shropshire in the papers from time to time, incurring the irritation of my friends. "Keep the place unspoilt" is their advice. But Shropshire is a secret too good to keep.

Shropshire lies at the heart of the Middle Marches of Wales, an English county cut neatly into two dissimilar halves by the great bend of the River Severn. To the north of Shrewsbury, the county town, lies the Shropshire Plain, a flat land with modest hills like those at Nesscliffe, country that shades imperceptibly into Cheshire. It is a land of Midland-Red brick cottages, great houses and orange cheese. South of the Severn we enter a different world. Long fingers of hills run north-east/south-west: the Longmynd, the Stretton Hills and The Wrekin; with the Wenlock Edge running as it does for 18 miles between Ironbridge (town and gorge have been declared a World Heritage Site) and Craven Arms. The two Clee Hills stand north to south and form a barrier between rural England and the Black Country. Travel across South Shropshire from east to west and the country changes from the Devonian-like red soil of the Clees and the Corve Dale to the limestone scarpes of the Wenlock Edge "forest-fleeced" as Housman put it), until the Longmynd, the Stiperstones, Cordon

STOKESAY CASTLE

Hill and the Clun Forest herald the coming of Wales. Between are the ranges of surprisingly dainty hills. It is a champaign county, green and gold, set in a frame of blue, pointed, distant hills.

The Welsh border is a country of great rivers, Severn, Teme, Wye and Usk. There are many others, Lugg, Onny, Corve and Clun, and they all have one thing in common. They flow west to east, coming out of the mountains of Wales into the English plain. There is but one exception, the River Camlad which flows from England into Wales by Chirbury on the extreme western edge of South Shropshire. It is curiously difficult to travel from east to west across South Shropshire. The principal road, the A49, runs north to south, the main artery between Liverpool and Manchester and Bristol and South Wales. Unless you want to jostle with juggernauts, avoid it, if you can. The railways

THE CLUN HILLS

run north to south too. The Great Western branch lines from Craven Arms to Wellington and Leominster to Kidderminster via Tenbury Wells have long since been torn up, their earthworks appearing almost as ancient as the Iron Age hill forts which crown the summits of nearly every hill on the Welsh Border.

There is a "B" road that runs from Church Stretton to Much Wenlock, and another which takes the traveller from Craven Arms up the southern slopes of the Wenlock Edge to Much Wenlock, but it is a hardy man indeed who would attempt to travel up the

Ape Dale from Wistanstow, or across and between the Clee Hills from Craven Arms or Diddlebury ("Delbury" to you). The lanes, wandering drunkenly between high hedges, offer tantalising views of distant hills and squat church towers (there are few church spires in Shropshire; towers were more easily built and adapted for defence against the marauders from Wales), and lead to muddy hamlets where the walls of barns still carry tinplate advertisements for Waverley Pens or yellow AA metal signs giving the number of miles to Cleobury Mortimer. There are pubs, but few if any of them resemble the Rover's Return. They are devoid of slot machines, plastic seats and juke boxes.

Shropshire has always been for me "the land of lost content" and Housman its poet. Housman was a Worcestershire lad who fell in love with an unknown Shropshire. As seen westwards from his home in Bromsgrove, the Clees were his "blue, remembered hills", a phrase which another writer, Denis Potter – who comes from the Forest of Dean – lifted for the title of one of his television plays. When Housman wrote *A Shropshire Lad* living in Highgate in the aftermath of an unrequited love affair with Moses Jackson, he plucked from the gazetteer such names as Ludlow, Clun and Wenlock for his melancholy, even morbid poems. I have no such excuse. My Shropshire love affairs have always been requited. Unlike A.E. Housman, I have been a frequent visitor to Shropshire. The poet, who sang so sweetly about

Wenlock Edge, where "the wood was troubled" and Abdon Burf which was "umbered" and Uricon where "the Roman slept", took care to spend his holidays in Venice in search of amorous escapades with gondoliers.

Nevertheless, love is love, whomsoever its object, and Housman's poetry has served to put Shropshire on the map. *A Shropshire Lad* has never been out of print since its publication in the 1890's, and a slim volume was carried in the breast pocket of every subaltern who went to Flanders. "Lads," as Housman would have put it, "of the 53rd" Who are the famous sons of Shropshire? Captain Matthew Webb was the first man to swim the English Channel, and for years his picture was to be found on boxes of matches. Lord Hill, who was Wellington's right hand man at Waterloo, stands on a Doric column in Shrewsbury. And we should not forget Clive of India and Admiral Benbow. Thomas Parr lived to be 153 years old. Perhaps he would have been alive today were it not for an ill-judged visit to the fleshpots of London. Wilfred Owen, the poet, was born at Oswestry and lived in Shrewsbury. Sir Gordon Richards, the jockey, was born at Oakengates. Benjamin Disraeli was the MP for Shrewsbury, while John Biffen, once Leader of the House, who lives at Llanyblodwell, became Conservative Member for North Shropshire in 1961.

"Shropshire" is a comfortable form of speech into which I can drop quite swiftly. John Betjeman in his Shell Guide to Shropshire claims that the English spoken between Shrewsbury and Clun is sometimes called the "Bishop's Castle Dialect". I have never heard it so described. The south Shropshire/North Hereford accent could be described as "Mummerset with Welsh intonations", Saxon with a Celtic lilt. The "h" is silent as in 'opesay, people say "'ow do?", and ambitious mothers warn their children that "you munna say dunna it inna perlite". There was once a Clee Hill dialect, a strange mixture owing to the influx of quarrymen and miners, but it has now disappeared.

Shropshire and the borders are a land to be enjoyed. Visit the great houses and take your Betjeman to church. Rummage in the antique shops of Ludlow and Leominster for early Staffordshire pots, and elderly barometers. Have lunch in pubs, and listen to the soft accents of the locals. Buy a clematis at Treasure's of Tenbury Wells and plant it in your suburban garden. Ask in Ludlow for the butcher's shop that sells the best sausages. Try to imagine what Shropshire and Hereford were like before the Great War when the gentry lived lives of leisure in great houses with servants, the farmers were all tenants, and the farm labourers struggled desperately to make ends meet. There was once no poverty like rural poverty. Since then, machinery has taken the place of the ploughman, and the comfortably retired have bought up, and tarted up, many of the cottages. The gentry have retreated into their houses.

LUDLOW

The great estates, like the Grove near Craven Arms where my uncles were estate workers, have been broken up, their tenants snapping up their cottages in the early 'fifties for what now appears to have been practically nothing. The juggernaut has displaced the train, and the motor car the horse; or, rather, the working horse. Distances have shrunk and dialects softened. But the beauty of the country remains: the tawny whale back of the Longmynd, the blue arrogance of the distant Clee, its back turned against the unkind Midlands, and lush, red lands of Hereford. Read Kilvert's diaries in bed, and Housman when you return home. But go quickly before it is too late, and Telford New Town absorbs all of Shropshire.

WOODS NEAR RICHARD'S CASTLE

CATTLE SALE, CRAVEN ARMS

BELOW
WENLOCK EDGE

EARLY MORNING, WENLOCK EDGE

CHAPTER 1

The centre of my childish world was Craven Arms, an ugly town, planted by the railway in the middle of the last century. But if Craven Arms is as plain as a traffic warden, it is situated plumb in the middle of the prettiest part of South Shropshire.

In its heyday, "the Arms" was a major junction on the old Great Western/LMS joint line between Shrewsbury and Hereford. Four or five times a day, the "Bristolian", Castle-hauled, thundered southwards at eighty miles an hour. It never stopped at Craven Arms. But, for those who wished, one line went deep into Central Wales, a single track to Swansea. Another followed the line of the Wenlock Edge to Wellington via Much Wenlock. It was closed in the 'fifties, long before Dr Beeching. The most bizarre was the Bishop's Castle Railway which ran twelve miles towards Newtown and Montgomery before expiring in a field. It closed down in 1936, its rails, or so I was told by my uncles, sold as scrap to the Germans, only to be returned by the Luftwaffe in the shape of bombs. My uncles, all three of whom had fought in Flanders, knew what they were talking about.

My uncle Campbell, whom I called Jack, was the head gardener at the Grove, an estate owned by a Mrs Harriet Greene, the widow of a former MP for Shrewsbury, and a distant kin of Graham Greene, the novelist. The Greenes owned much of Wistanstow and Leamore Common, including the maternal cottage. Jack's brother, Oscar, was a game-keeper on the estate.

On the morning of Sunday, September 3, 1939, I remember, the wireless was taken into the garden and we sat and listened to Neville Chamberlain's broadcast. He seemed strangely peevish, as if Herr Hitler had behaved badly to spite him. My uncle and aunt were silent; their only son was of military age. My cousin Edna in her teens was more cheerful.

She told us all that the initials KSLI stood not for the King's Shropshire Light Infantry (A.E. Housman's "the 53rd") but, when reversed, "I Love Soldiers' Kisses". I was only eight, but I laughed politely along with the rest.

Craven Arms — with its sheep market, railway station and cinema, the owner of which, a Mr Robson, drove a Rolls-Royce — may not have been much to write home about, but it could lay claim to Stokesay Castle, a fortified manor house so prettily appointed as to be worthy of the better kind of chocolate box. As a castle, it is a paper tiger, its tower and castellation an elaborate bluff, a gesture towards the border violence of the post-Norman conquest. It was built in 1280 by a Ludlow merchant grown rich off the backs of sheep. The castle, and its gatehouse, together with a church rebuilt and refurnished in the style of the Protectorate, lie midway between two bluffs where the river Onny cuts below Wenlock Edge. It can be glimpsed from the A49, but a better view can be obtained from the window of a passing train. The castle is uninhabited, but well preserved, and open to visitors.

John Betjeman, in his Shell Guide to Shropshire, describes Wistanstow as "a secluded but not very pretty village", although he is kind about the cruciform church. The village is called after St Wystan.

I was sent to the village school, a nervous child with a piping West London accent, planted here to avoid Hitler's bombs. The headmaster kindly put me in the girls' half for my protection. He was wise. Once the final afternoon bell had rung, Rosemary Price, the daughter of a neighbour in whose care I had been placed, and I ran for our lives up the lane towards Leamore Common and safety, pursued by Shropshire Lads crying "rotten taters". It was my first taste of the mob.

It was not so much my ordeal but my accent — which had quickly acquired a Shropshire tinge — that compelled my mother to pay a flying visit. Had she not spent many years ridding herself of hers? It was then that I was sent to Brockhurst at Church Stretton where the English was standard and the conditions Spartan. There I was thumped for talking Shropshire.

My uncle's cottage faced the Wenlock Edge and Flounder's Folly, a tower which had been built in 1838 on the 1000ft summit of Callow Hill. On a fine day, or so I was told, you could see the sea. We called it the Monument. It is today owned by Julie Christie, along with some ancient woods.

With our backs to the Longmynd, we seemed cut off from the world to the east by ranges of hills. Behind the Wenlock Edge, a heavily wooded escarpment 18 miles long, lay the peaks of the two Clees, the Brown and Titterstone which my uncle asserted was the highest land between Shropshire and the Urals. I was mightily impressed although as much could be said for the Gog and Magog Hills outside Cambridge.

But the Clees and 20 miles of bad roads still protect Shropshire from the Black Country. The reason for the radar station on top of the Titterstone Clee, it is said, is to alert the shopkeepers of Ludlow to the arrival of trippers from Brum. Geologists — and Shropshire is a county of geologists — claim that the Longmynd is pre-Cambrian, and as such made of the oldest sedimentary rocks in England and Wales.

The Longmynd is separated from the Stretton Hills by a narrow fault-line through which ran the Roman road from Uriconium to Magna via Bravonium which is now Leintwardine. The A49 has been built on top of it.

I was packed off to Brockhurst School in the winter of 1940/41. I began as a weekly boarder in September '40, an unsatisfactory arrangement which meant catching the eight o'clock bus (Midland Red, single decker with a silver roof) at the corner of Bushmoor lane. Pitch dark and freezingly cold mornings waiting for the bright lights of the bus to appear at Felhampton were an unhappy prelude to a week of rigorous discomfort. The headmaster of Brockhurst was an ex Osborne naval instructor called R.P. Marshall ("RPM" for short) who was terrifying. The dorms were called after admirals, the staff were as old as the hills, and the headmaster had the nasty habit of throwing small boys who had not learnt to swim into the deep end of the open-air pool as an exercise in building character. He had been forced to make one concession to the prurient of the Long Mynd Hotel. Where once we swam, or sank, naked, we were obliged to wear slips so as not to offend the susceptibilities of the guests who must, on reflection, have been remarkably long-sighted.

Perhaps there is something prudish about Church Stretton. The original village grew rapidly in the last years of Queen Victoria, turning into a resort town ("Little Switzerland") but a century too late for a spa. Stretton water is now bottled and the fluid in which I bathed while at Brockhurst is now sold in supermarkets at the litre-price of petrol. Church Stretton has many late Victorian villas, the last stop on life's journey for a legion of Cheshire tradesmen. It is a town of lace curtains, monkey puzzles and undistinguished shops.

But there are echoes in the town of a less repressive past. The north door of St Lawrence's church has a "sheela na gig" set into the wall above it. Sheelas are thought to be of Celtic origin, which does not fit with the Norman and early English origins of the church. They are what well brought up small children would call "rude", a crude representation of a female figure exposing her private parts to the local bourgeois. How can it have survived the scrutiny of priest and pastor? To say nothing of the parsons' wives?

The church has a "Jessica window" in memory of a Stretton woman called Heba Stretton whose Victorian novel *Jessica's First Prayer* (1866) sold several million copies. To today's eyes it must be unreadable. I would prefer the other Stretton publication written the year before by the rector of nearby Woolstaston called *A Night in the Snow*. The good rector was caught in a blizzard and wandered the Longmynd for 24 hours until the storm lifted. He narrowly escaped death.

The Church Stretton November Fair used to be called "Dead Men's Fair", owing to the deaths that occurred on the Longmynd from a combination of drunkenness and exposure. The hills brood over the town, a threatening presence particularly in winter.

Professor Richard Cobb claims Caradoc to be the most elegant hill in Shropshire, but I prefer the Titterstone Clee when seen from the Fiddler's Elbow on the road between Bromfield and Leintwardine. Carding Mill Valley is a popular tourist spot, too trippery for the more fastidious. Ashes Valley which runs into the Longmynd from Little Stretton, a pretty place with two good pubs, the Ragleth and the Green Dragon, to which the weary assistant masters of Brockhurst would go to escape from the headmaster and the tiresome boys, is much more attractive.

Climb the path that follows the stream until the summit of the Mynd is reached. Take a good book; lie in the sun and sleep to awaken to a view over Housman's coloured counties that can stretch, if rain is threatened, to the distant Malvern Hills and the green lands of Hereford. The self-indulgent might take a walkman and play Elgar, a Worcestershire man who wrote of "the sweet borderland" that lies between England and Wales.

The more adventurous visitor to Stretton could drive his motor car along the Burway, the single-tracked pathway which leads from the town on to the Portway and then down the steeper western scarp of the Longmynd which overlooks Cordon Hill and the Stiperstones. He, or she, will need strong nerves for the climb and descent are dangerous with a precipice on one's right hand.

On the top of the Mynd the road divides, the right fork leading more gently down to Ratlinghope (pronounced "Ratchup"), a forgotten village in the back of beyond. But from Ratchup there is a secondary road that leads to Shrewsbury via Cathercott, relatively free of traffic and with a most spectacular view over the North Shropshire and Cheshire Plain with The Wrekin to the east and the line of the Berwyns to the west. Those on the Mynd who turn left, and drive easily along the Portway as far as the gliders, must then plunge down the steepest track in Shropshire, hoping against hope that the route is clear. The brave are rewarded for the country that lies immediately to the west of the Longmynd is remote and totally unspoilt.

There is much more to the Longmynd than Church Stretton. The mountain is ringed by attractive villages such as Cardington with its church and circular churchyard, a sign, so it is believed, of a pagan place of worship. The early Christians were astute enough to incorporate the festivals of their converts, and to make use of their religious sites.

Minton is a curious hamlet that archaeologists say has retained to this day the "open plan" of a Saxon settlement. But it is the Mynd itself that dominates the surrounding country. Dark in winter, green in summer, windy, lonely and bleak, it is, because of its unimaginable age, the Great Survivor. It has seen us all come and go.

FARM AT PLOWDEN HILL

RIVER ONNY VALLEY FROM THE PORTWAY

SUN-UP AT ENCHMARSH

FEBRUARY ON THE LONGMYND

DAWN OVER CAER CARADOC

THE STRETTON HILLS, EVENING

NEAR ASTERTON IN THE ONNY VALLEY

LOOKING SOUTH NEAR MYNDTON

THE VILLAGE OF CARDINGTON

FLOUNDERS FOLLY, WENLOCK EDGE

SUNSET OVER LONGMYND

WINTER TREES AT WISTANSTOW

AUTUMN ON WENLOCK EDGE

COOT AT STOKESAY

A SALOPIAN REMEMBERS: SHREWSBURY

THE ENGLISH BRIDGE, SHREWSBURY

CHAPTER 2

I have always had mixed feelings about Shrewsbury, the school that is, not the town. I was sent to Shrewsbury in January 1945 for no good reason. We were living near Bristol and my father, resplendent in his naval uniform, accompanied me by train. The view from the carriage window was familiar enough: the "high-reared head of Clee" as we passed Ludlow; my uncle Arnold's village shop which could be glimpsed as we rattled over the level crossing at Onibury, and the desolate and lonely Wistanstow Halt. I can remember my fear, the smell of which must have mingled with the reek of buttoned carriage cloth.

Shrewsbury School is a public school founded by the pious King Edward VI in 1552. It had risen during the 19th century under a succession of formidable headmasters to the status of a Clarendon School, one of the country's top five public schools.

Small boys accept the buffetings of fate as their due, an ill-formed concept of what is fair or unfair providing an inadequate measure of the inevitable rough justice, and scant protection against it. I do not want to give a wrong impression. I was unhappy for only part of the time. Luckily, I was tough enough not to be bullied, and high spirits enabled us all to make the best of what was, all too often, a bad job.

The School was, in my day, an Arnoldian fortress built on a bluff overlooking the Quarry and the town. We had the best view possible of the spires of Shrewsbury which is, according to Housman, "islanded in Severn stream". There are, I believe, ten bridges of all sorts and sizes over the Severn in the vicinity of Shrewsbury, but the School had its own, Kingsland bridge, which still charges a toll of a copper or two to cross. The School site is large, and the individual houses are scattered across it. I was put in Oldham's Hall, or Sopwith's, which was

the name of its housemaster.

I was swiftly reminded of the correct way to pronounce Shrewsbury. The more or less educated call Shropshire's county town "Shrosebury"; hoi polloi call it much as it is spelt. In my youth the aged country people spoke of "going to Salop for the day". Maybe they still do, but I doubt it. I had no trouble with "Shrewsbury" but a good deal with the School and House colours which all "new scum" were obliged to learn on pain of corporal punishment. Sopwith's colours were chocolate and gold, or were they chocolate and white?

Shrewsbury itself provided a backdrop to life at school, a comfort, a reminder that there was, in fact, life beyond the school. On Saturday afternoons during term we were sometimes allowed "down town", having won permission from the housemaster. The reasons required were sufficiently trivial – a watch repaired, a new pair of shoes, a book to be collected from Smiths – to suggest a blind eye. Unfortunately these visits were cut short by a roll-call held at four o'clock. We were thus permitted two separate periods of 90 minutes; 180 would have been enough to sneak into the cinema near the station to see Margaret Lockwood and James Mason in *The Wicked Lady*. I did manage to see it, but in two, disjointed halves. It was not until years later that I saw the complete film late at night on BBC2.

In 1947 I could run from the school to the cinema in less than ten minutes. My God, how fit we were. Several times a term the whole school would turn out on a cross country run. My main memory of three and a half undistinguished years is of running for my life through the mud and filth of some Shropshire farmyard, pursued by savage dogs. Nevertheless, my fitness lasted into middle life, a consequence, no doubt, of so much obligatory exercise.

In the late 'forties, Salopians (I use the word to describe town and gown) walked past the market hall, a late Victorian horror which only John Betjeman could love, with eyes averted. To make way for this red and blue-bricked monstrosity, magnificent timber-framed buildings in Shoplatch and Claremont Street had been demolished in 1866. It was, in its turn, demolished only to be replaced by a 'fifties horror. Even so there was, and still is, enough of the mediaeval and Georgian town left to enchant hordes of visitors.

The charm of Shrewsbury lies in its ancient buildings and crooked streets. It is a town of great churches but it has no Anglican cathedral, the "proud Salopians" of the past having refused a Bishop. Shropshire is still divided between the bishoprics of Lichfield and Hereford. St Mary's has one of the tallest spires in England. St Alkmund has a unique dedication to a Saxon saint, and has been visited by the devil. A contemporary account reads as follows: "This year, 1553, upon the 12th day in Shrewsbury, the Devil appeared in St Alkmund's church and there when the priest was at High Mass, with great tempest and darkness, so that he passed through the church he mounted up the steeple in the said church, tearing the wires of the said clock, and put the print of his claws upon the fourth bell and took one of the pinnacles away with him, and for the time stayed all the bells in the churches within the said town so that they would neither toll nor ring. This visitation followed closely upon an outbreak of the sweating sickness which spread from Shrewsbury all over England. It attacked people when they were eating, sleeping, praying or laughing, and caused death within the hour."

How peaceful the town has since become.

St Chad's, at the top of the town, is round Georgian, stout and much decorated.

The past wealth of Shrewsbury, founded upon wool, is still evident in the black and white timbered houses of the Rowleys, the Owens and the Irelands, mediaeval magnates whose mansions still stand. Rowley's Mansion is now the town's museum, with a stock of Roman remains taken from nearby Uriconium – once Britain's fourth largest city, which is to this day, largely unexcavated.

The headmaster of Shrewsbury in the late 'forties was John Wolfenden, later to win fame as the author of the famous report on homosexuality. He sat like a constitutional monarch over a "cabinet" of housemasters, who had, in their turn, shuffled off their responsibilities for discipline onto the backs of the house monitors and school praeposters. The houses were tyrannies ruled by 18-year-olds. Cold baths, chapel, as well as games were compulsory. The cold baths – we broke the ice on them in the winter – did not stop us thinking about sex, although the subject of girls was frowned upon as not being quite manly. Chapel did, at least, have the benefit of relative privacy. The services were long, and frequent.

My hobby was train-spotting. On Sunday afternoons I would go down to the railway station and spend time upon its deserted platforms. A friend, called Platts, took photographs of Castles, Halls and Stanier's Black Fives. This passion for steam lasted until I plucked up courage to buy a copy of *Health and Efficiency* from the station bookstall. I then took to bicycling across the country, leaving "the site" at one-thirty to return at six. In this way we explored Shropshire within a radius of 18 or so miles, climbing to the top of The Wrekin, taking Telford's road to the caves at Nesscliffe and scoffing eggs and bacon in a pub, pedalling south-east to Much Wenlock with its stiff climb up the Edge, or south to Pontesbury Hill and the Longmynd. The roads on Sundays in the late 'forties were empty, and the prevailing westerly winds blew us smartly back to school in time for tea.

It was at Shrewsbury that I read Mary Webb's *Gone to Earth*. She was more than "a Shropshire novelist", she could be said to have invented "the Shropshire School". Her novels, which enjoyed such a vogue in the 'twenties and 'thirties thanks to a posthumous plug by the then Prime Minister, Stanley Baldwin, owed something to Thomas Hardy and a little to the Brontes. They were romantic to the verge of parody. Nevertheless they are not without charm.

Precious Bane, probably her best book, is set in the lake country of north-west Shropshire around Ellesmere. But the real Mary Webb country is the Stiperstones, a line of hills rising to 1700 feet and topped with tors of quartzite, the most prominent of which is the Devil's Chair. When shrouded by cloud the Devil is in residence. "He be in his chair", mothers warn their children. Hazel Woodus, the heroine of *Gone to Earth* plunges to her death down the shaft of a disused lead mine, pursued by the South Shropshire Hunt. The story is allegorical. Evil is symbolised by the lusts of Squire Reddin: good by an earnest young preacher who was too scrupulous to consummate his marriage. There is an awful lot of hot breath and purple prose, and rainstorms are forever battering upon cottage windows. Her books contain a good deal of Shropshire dialect which my experiences at Wistanstow village school allowed me to decipher.

Poor Mary Webb; her reputation was destroyed by a single book by another author, Stella Gibbons's *Cold Comfort Farm*, that wicked take-off of rural passion. Yet Mary Webb's Shropshire still remains.

The Longmynd is Shropshire's Magic Mountain. Sixty square miles of tableland, rising to a height of 1700ft, the Mynd is white in the winter, dark-green where the Forestry Commission has laid its Swedish fingers, brown in the autumn when the bracken is shrivelled, and blue when glimpsed from a distance. It is the Salopian's playground, and bronzed Mancunians in El Alamein shorts stride across the mountain, Guardian in pocket and map in hand. The Portway, a pre-historic trackway, bends between the tumuli of ancient warrior kings, and lovers lie back upon the springy turf, oblivious to the spreading stain of whinberries.

At school at Shrewsbury, I could glimpse the northern edge of the Mynd from the bedroom window in my house. I would sit on the sill reading *Gone to Earth* and dreaming of randy squires pursuing comely virgins across the county. In Powell and Pressburger's film of the book, shot in 1947, Squire Reddin (Derek Farrar) is seen riding across the top of the Mynd in search of Jennifer Jones. I was never as lucky.

In the 18th century the gentry acquired town houses in Shrewsbury in which to spend the season. This resulted in the happy development of handsome Georgian houses flanked by spacious gardens in Belmont. A walk to St Chad's up St John's Hill and back, by almost any route you like to the English bridge, will reveal Georgian houses and crescents, hidden gardens and surprising views. Shrewsbury is a hill town and The Wrekin is ever present. The Quarry consists of public gardens which owe much to the skill of Percy Thrower, and the paths are lined with avenues of lime trees.

The 19th century laid but a light finger on Shrewsbury. The industrial revolution which began 12 miles away in Coalbrookdale moved swiftly elsewhere, and the county town largely escaped the red brick with which the century disfigured much of England. On market day, the town is packed with farmers' wives in Doris Archer hats stocking up for the week at the multiple stores. Shrewsbury is, together with Chester, an unofficial capital of Wales, so poor are the north/south communications in the Principality. It has always been easier for a North Walian to come to Shrewsbury than to struggle south to Cardiff.

At Shrewsbury School we were taught the names of famous Old Salopians, including Sir Philip Sidney upon whom we were encouraged to model ourselves. Had he not given a drink of water to a dying soldier when terribly wounded himself? The town of Shrewsbury is twinned with Zutphen, the site of the battle. There was also Darwin, about whom, for some reason much less was said. Will any of my contemporaries become famous Old Salopians? I can suggest only two: Michael Heseltine, and Richard Ingrams the satirist.

Elsewhere I have described how Michael and I took our revenge on Shrewsbury in 1952. I wangled

an invitation for us to return to propose and second a motion "that this House would abolish the public schools". After a hectic debate in which home truths flew like confetti, the motion, in scenes reminiscent of the worst excesses of the French Revolution, was carried by one vote. I retired to my hotel, Michael stayed with Mr Phillips, his old housemaster. Flushed with victory, I telephoned the Press Association, gave them a breathless account of what had happened, and the news of a great public school voting to abolish itself appeared in every paper. Michael came down to breakfast in Moser's Hall quite unabashed and proceeded to upbraid Phillips over the cornflakes on the topic of juvenile homosexuality. Mrs Phillips was driven from the room.

The Old Salopian Society threatened immediate expulsion. There was much shaking of grey Salopian heads and it was opined that Michael Heseltine would come to no good end.

SHREWSBURY SCHOOL

THE QUARRY, SHREWSBURY

PRINCESS STREET, SHREWSBURY

FEBRUARY, NEAR BICTON

IRONBRIDGE POWER STATION

THE BRIDGE, IRONBRIDGE

WHITEMERE, SOUTH OF ELLESMERE

ST CHAD'S CHURCH & ST JOHN'S HILL

IRONBRIDGE POWER STATION

THE RIVER SEVERN AT SHREWSBURY

BLAKEMERE IN WINTER

THE WREKIN

FARM COTTAGE AT WROXETER

ON THE WELSH BORDER

MOEL Y GOLFA, WEST OF SHREWSBURY

CHAPTER 3

The Welsh Border includes by definition the old border counties of Montgomery and Radnor. The border between England and Wales (or between the English and the British as the Celtic inhabitants of Britannia were driven remorselessly into their western mountain fastnesses by the Saxon invaders, in the years after the legions had been recalled to Rome) was finally fixed in 1536 under the Tudors when the Council of the Marches with its seat at Ludlow Castle was abolished. Much of what is now Wales was once in Shropshire as was Montgomery itself, a Norman-planted town and the seat of the county.

An older frontier was Offa's Dyke or Ditch, built by the Mercians in the Dark Ages; today the border with Wales swings either side of "the great ditch."

The 1536 settlement seems as capricious as the more recent border between Northern Ireland and the South. Church Stoke and the Corndon, a sinister-looking, volcanic hill north of Bishop's Castle were put into Wales; the Clun Forest, where most of the place names are Welsh, remained inside Shropshire. I suppose it was a matter of who had clout at court. The Welsh-speaking hill country west of Oswestry stayed in England. The border itself is unimportant. As with all borderlands the two counties merge imperceptibly marked only by a subtle change in the surface of the road or by a brave sign in both English and Welsh.

My mother's family were called Morris, Evans and Jones, but they did not consider themselves to be Welsh. They had been born the "right" side of Offa's Dyke and were Shropshire folk. As they were also Anglicans, they voted Conservative. The Welsh, who were Nonconformist, voted Liberal. The Welsh also tended, as do the Catholics of Fermanagh to this day, to live and farm above the thousand-foot contour mark. The Welsh border is a land of riches. Take

the clapped-out diesel train, which runs from Craven Arms on the Central Wales line to Llandridnod Wells and Swansea, at least as far as Knighton (the station is in England; the town in Wales), and you will travel through an unspoilt part of Shropshire. Clungunford is a pretty village, while away to the west lies the village of Hopton where stands the 14th-century keep of a Norman castle, the scene of a Civil War atrocity when 24 Parliamentarians were mutilated and then done to death by the Royalists. It now seems an unlikely place for such horrors.

Hopton lies at the entrance of a valley which leads into the Clun Forest and the other Caer Caradoc which has a hill fort on its summit. After many twists and turns, the lane meets eventually the main road from Knighton to Clun, but not before passing through some of the wildest country in Shropshire. The back of beyond begins at Hopton. Opposite the village, to the east, is a vale bordered by the extension of Wenlock Edge, the hills thus enclosing the valley, railway and B class roads, an Arcadia where the water is still unpolluted, the air fresh, and chickens are permitted the liberty of the farmyard.

The vale of Hopton — it is not called that, but ought to be — merges, via Leintwardine, into the Vale of Wigmore, which is its proper title. Leintwardine is now in Hereford, but was once in Shropshire. It is the Roman Bravonium, a military post on the Roman road which ran from Uriconium, now Wroxeter, to Magnis, now Kenchester near Hereford. Aged natives call it "Lenterdin", and it is the fictional birthplace of Dr Bradley, the hero of a famous novel called *Dr Bradley Remembers* by a long-forgotten author, Francis Brett Young.

Two roads run westwards from Craven Arms into Wales. The more northerly leaves the A49 at the Grove with its captive army of doomed battery chickens, and follows the river Onny through Horderley and Plowden to Bishop's Castle and beyond. The other joins the Shrewsbury to Hereford main road at the Craven Arms Hotel where there stands a mile post erected before the building of Telford's new and improved London to Holyhead road. This is the road to Clun and beyond, a backroad into Wales which rises steadily as it climbs to the top of the Clun Forest and then plunges down into the valley of the Severn, to Newtown and mid-Wales.

I doubt if anyone ever goes to Wales this way. The road seems empty, and what traffic there is peters out when you get to Clun itself which is a large village with a ruined castle and a handsome church. Although no railway ever made it to Clun, Clun gives the visitor the strong impression of being at the end of the line. It lies between high hills, many of which have pre-historic camps on their tops, hidden beneath caps of the Forestry Commission's pines. The motorist is tempted to turn either to the north or to the south, to Knighton or to Bishop's Castle; it takes courage to continue to the west which seems somehow to be threatening. The castle was clearly built to keep the Welsh out of the fat lands of Shropshire and how vulnerable and lonely an outpost it must have once been. But persevere. The valley widens between Clun and Newcastle, the road cutting across one of the best stretches of Offa's Dyke.

After Newcastle, where there is a comfortable pub called the Crown, the road climbs steeply to the Anchor Inn, past a hill-farm once owned by Peter Walker in the years before he became Minister of Agriculture. He sold out and went to live in Worcester.

The Clun Forest is summer country. Life must be hard from the end of October to the beginning of May. Snow, when it falls, lingers long beneath the hedges. The return of the sun brings out the city walker, many of whom follow the line of Offa's Dyke in a pilgrimage, the full extension of which should take them from the Bristol Channel to the Irish Sea. There is a saying in Clun that as soon as you have crossed the bridge your wits are sharpened, but it is not clear in which direction. I suspect east to west. The old Saxon part of Clun is near the church; the Normans, who built the castle, "planted" the rest.

There is a small museum which contains thousands of flint arrowheads, knives and scrapers, evidence of the existence of an ancient trade route which, keeping to the tops of the hills, crossed South Shropshire in the direction of the river Severn at Bewdley.

The valleys would have been swampy and wooded, only the uplands would have been comparatively free of shrubs and trees. The Shropshire hills which have become partly wooded since the end of the Kaiser's War, thanks to the need to become self-sufficient in timber, were once bare, cropped by sheep. In pre-historic times they would have been lightly covered with scrub oak.

In these parts the gentry, par excellence, are the Mores. In 1977 I was invited by Jasper More, the MP for Ludlow, to speak to a weekend school held by the Ludlow constituency Young Conservatives. MPs are the frequent victims of invitations of this kind as constituency political activity, but the attraction with this case was that it carried with it an invitation to spend two nights with Clare and Jasper More at Linley Hall, the Palladian mansion which Jasper had reoccupied after the war in the name of his ancestors. The invitation was irresistible. He was a friend, and as important perhaps was my wish to be the first member of my family to sleep under the roof of Linley, the guest of a More. During the centuries in which one More after another had been "the

Member" for Ludlow, my ancestors (not the sort with portraits) voted for them. If a cat could look at a king, a "Morris" could dine with a More.

The Mores are Shropshire gentry on a par with the Heber Percys, the Plowdens, the Ormsby Gores and the Windsor-Clives. (The Earl of Shrewsbury lives in Staffordshire.) They own great houses, but not the kind that have private zoos. Linley Hall faces south east, its back to the foothills of the Stiperstones, looking out towards the western wall of the Longmynd. Jasper More was the last of the Tory party's "library squires", a tall cultured man with the most exquisite manners. He wrote a book called *"A Tale of Two Houses"*, a beautifully written account of the Mores' return to a barely habitable Linley, the house having passed out of the ownership of the family owing to money troubles. Clare and Jasper More together renovated the great house, restored the gardens, and put the estate on a sound footing. In his book there are copies of letters that passed between Jasper More's father and Stanley Baldwin. More complains of the trippers who had knocked down gates on his land as their charabancs (in the 'thirties the word "coach" was reserved for trains and stages) sought out the beauties of the Mary Webb country.

Stanley Baldwin, whose praise of Mary Webb a year or so before had made the author fashionable, replied wryly from Downing Street: *"The unforeseen results of my remarks on Mary Webb have been a lesson to me … I can only hope that in time you may forgive though you may never forget."*

Baldwin who, like Housman, was a Worcestershire man, had a similar passion for Shropshire, the county whence his ancestors had come. In the 'twenties and 'thirties he would, as Prime Minister, take walking holidays through the Marches, staying, unrecognised, at country pubs. There were then no detectives; no television interviews, no "sound bites". How we have changed, and not always for the better.

The main town in these parts is Bishop's Castle, but it has never been the same since the Great Reform Bill of 1832. Until then the town returned two MPs to Parliament, indeed, in 1820 four candidates polled 87 votes each, and as no provision had been made for a casting vote, they were all returned to parliament. In the 1950s, with a population of 1300, it still had a Mayor, four Aldermen and 12 Councillors.

If Clun is a village with pretensions, Bishop's Castle is a town which has seen better days. There is a long High Street which climbs to the site of the castle, and, as would be expected, the better houses are at the top of the town. Today it has no MPs, no Mayor, no mace, and no railway. But it does have some handsome Georgian houses, an Old Market House and Town Hall and an ancient pub, the Three Tuns, where the landlord brews his own beer.

Even at the end of the 1980s, Bishop's Castle showed few, if any, signs of gentrification, the tendency for the rich and retired to take refuge in small country towns, and to bring with them the boutiques, delicatessens and Good Food Guide restaurants which are now to be found in places like Dorrington and Ludlow. In consequence, the cost of property is lower than elsewhere. Bishop's Castle is quiet enough to suit even A.E. Housman, save perhaps on Fridays, Market Day, and the views over the surrounding country from the top of the town are very fine – to the north, Corndon and the tors of the Stiperstones, to the east the Longmynd, and to the south the broken hill country of south-west Shropshire. Only to the west is the view blocked by the hills of the Clun Forest.

An inhabitant of Bishop's Castle could shop in Shrewsbury, eat in Clun and sleep in the summer sun.

DISUSED CHAPEL, CLUNGUNFORD

HOPTON CASTLE

THE CLUN VALLEY

MIDDLETON HILL, LOOKING EAST INTO SHROPSHIRE

THE DEVIL'S CHAIR, STIPERSTONES HILL

RATLINGHOPE

LINLEY HALL

THE CLOCKTOWER, BISHOP'S CASTLE

THE RIVER CLUN AT HURST

STUBBLE AT LITTLE BRAMPTON

CLUN AND THE CLUN VALLEY

BARLEY FIELD NEAR ASTON ON CLUN

CLUN CASTLE

LLANFAIR HILL, ABOVE THE CLUN VALLEY

WINDOWLEDGE, CLUNTON

THE CLEE HILLS
AND LUDLOW

BODENHAM'S, LUDLOW

CHAPTER 4

When I was a child living in Leamore Common with my uncle and aunt, I learnt that the Brown Clee Hill was 1792 feet high, only eight feet short of a mountain. If that were not disappointment enough, the other Clee, the handsome one with an aquiline profile, which appeared to be so much higher, was only 1749 feet above sea level. With the obsessiveness of childhood I made a list of the heights of other famous Shropshire peaks. The Stiperstones were in the 1700s, the Longmynd, 1696. Caradoc was only 1500, while The Wrekin, around which peak all Shropshire toasted itself ("All friends round The Wrekin") was a mere 1300. Later, I discovered that the Brown Clee had lost its top, blasted away by quarrymen in the last century. The peak of Titterstone has been preserved by its owner, the Earl of Plymouth, who wished not to spoil the view from his seat at Oakly Park, near Bromfield. Mercifully, the Clee Hill has been left – if not intacta, for the quarrying for dhu stone (road stone) continues apace – at least virga from Lord Plymouth's windows.

It is not hard to drive to the peak of the Titterstone Clee Hill for there is a road of sorts that leads from the village on the main road through the ravaged landscape, skirting the edge of quarries, until the peak itself is but a short climb on foot.

In the summer of 1960 I climbed it properly from the northern approaches, sheltering deep in the bracken from a sudden rainstorm. The view from the summit is perhaps the finest in south Shropshire. I can recall a massing of purple thunderheads, the blue of distant hills spread out in a panorama, and the bright green and gold of a thousand fields. The wind blew steadily from Wales, from Radnor Forest and the distant Black Mountains, Kilvert Country. To the south lay the Malverns, home of genteel widows and music festivals, and beyond, a faint smudge on the south eastern horizon, the line of the Cotswolds where every village has its minor Royal and the Rovers are all Range.

The Clees preside over the richest part of Shropshire. To the east the country shades into the Forest of Wyre. Cleobury Mortimer ("Clibbery") is a pretty village astride the main road with Georgian houses and a church with a wooden, twisted spire. Mawley Hall, near Cleobury, is the most handsome Georgian house, built in 1730 for Sir Edward Blunt, while Burwarton Hall, near Cleobury North, is the home of Lord Boyne. There has been only a modest amount of development, and the village has been spared a rash of bungalows, an infection which is spreading across the Welsh Marches. The bungalow is an abomination; I have never seen one which I coveted. Clive of India was a Shropshire man, but, by bringing the bungalow back from the sub-continent, he did no one a favour. They seem to bring the depressing style of urban retirement into rural England, shades of Edgbaston darkening Housman's Shropshire.

Michael Raven in his Shropshire Gazetteer, tells of a witch who lived in Cleobury North called Prissy Morris who had the power to stop a horse dead in its tracks, a power possessed by a famous woman politician of my acquaintance.

To the west of the Clees is Corve Dale where the lanes are sunken and the villages, remote. All that remains of the village of Heath is its Norman chapel which stands alone in a field around which can still be traced the outlines of long-vanished cottages, and a stone-lined well. The Black Death, a cold climate and agricultural depression have all taken their toll. The chapel has neither tower nor belfry. Barn-like, with slitted windows and box pews, there is a smell of damp hymn books, neglect and sanctity.

Not far away is Holdgate, another shrunken village living on its past glories. Fritz Holgot entertained King Henry I in 1109, and the ruined tower of his castle lies behind a farm. The church is particularly fine: it is fortress-like, as are many Shropshire churches, and contains carvings of the Hereford School, the most spectacular survivals of which are to be found at Kilpeck, south-west of Hereford. Like the church at Church Stretton, it, too, has a sheela-na-gig, whose pagan fertility symbolism the early Christians were loth to abandon.

Today's fertility symbols are the blue silage towers which stand like so many inter-continental ballistic missiles in the farmyards of the Corve Dale.

The "capital" of the dale is Much Wenlock which bears the same relationship to Craven Arms as Washington does to New York. Wenlock is a one-eyed hole of much charm. It also has several calls to fame. The ruined abbey dates from 680 when it was founded by the first king of Magonsaete, the name given for Shropshire south of the Severn and the Herefordshire plain. (The division of the county into the dioceses of Lichfield and Hereford dates from the same period.) The Prior's Lodge, built in 1500, survived the dissolution in 1539 and is now a magnificent private house. Norma Major was born in Wenlock. But the town has made but one public appearance. In 1947 it became part of Powell and Pressburger's *Gone to Earth*, the film whose charms for me I have already mentioned. Jennifer Jones and a very young George Cole were filmed outside the Market Hall with the unpaid help of most of the town's inhabitants.

Much Wenlock stands at one end of Corve Dale. At the other is Ludlow – "the most beautiful small town in England". Ludlow has its own poet. Alfred Housman once said that he picked Shropshire as the object of his affection for the magic of its names: Wenlock, Clun and Clee – and the rivers Teme and Onny, while he made Ludlow, the town towards which his doomed lads were always striding on May mornings, the capital of his "land of lost content". The Shropshire of a century ago, when Housman was a schoolboy in Bromsgrove, was a rural backwater remote even from the rapidly growing centres of Midlands industry. Its people were united by poverty and deference to parson, squire and preacher. The younger men no longer wore the smock and beaver hat. The more prosperous farmers had built their farms in fields away from the villages, handsome red-brick houses, the mark of the agricultural prosperity of the French wars, a prosperity that was not to last. The gentry wintered in Ludlow in splendid Georgian houses in Broad, Corve and Mill Streets.

It was from this land, or the idea of it, that the adolescent Housman drew comfort and refreshment. His early childhood was idyllic. A timid and intro-spective child, he was the eldest of seven. His father was a solicitor and incompetent; his mother, who died when Alfred was twelve, was an intelligent woman, the daughter of a Gloucester parson. Her death was probably for Housman the most traumatic event in a lifetime full of personal disasters. He was homosexual. Those to whom Housman gave his love either did not survive, or could not return it. It is this which accounts for his bitter lyricism and profound pessimism; and it was into that magic yet unvisited land, the hills of which would have been lit up by the sunsets of his childhood, that he poured his discontents.

That is the land of lost content
I see it shining plain
The happy highways where I went
And cannot come again

Ludlow, which was not so very long ago a bit dilapidated, has spruced itself up in the last twenty years, its inhabitants having been augmented by the environmentally-conscious middle-class. It is a stately town, planted by the Normans in the lee of the castle, and beautified in the 18th century by the local gentry. It is still relatively remote, although the number of bridges thrown across the river Severn has increased recently, and the tourists are much in evidence. Thank God, the Clee Hills and twenty miles of unsatisfactory roads still lie between Ludlow and the Black Country commuter.

Ludlow has never lacked admirers, including Professor Joad who asserted on the wireless that Ludlow is the most beautiful small town in England, and, indeed, it is hard to list its rivals. Perhaps Stamford, Rye, and Richmond, Yorkshire, would be contenders for the apple.

Ludlow is exactly the right size. It is small, compact and harmonious. There are signs that it may not be long before it becomes chi-chi, as bogus as such Surrey towns as Farnham where the front doors are all painted a pastel pink and even the policemen talk posh. This tendency should be guarded against, but I am not certain how. But in Ludlow most people still think a jacuzzi to be a breed of dog.

Ludlow is every bit as much a hill town as anything that can be found in Tuscany. It is caught in the crook of the river Teme, a warren of narrow streets, packed with pubs, farriers and antique dealers, people who came for the day thirty years ago from Manchester and Birmingham, and stayed. The Feathers is a spectacular Tudor hotel of the kind that is patronised by visiting Americans who look like Cary Grant.

The local Tory party has its dingy offices in a Georgian house in Broad Street fit for a Surrey stockbroker, and Dinham Hall, a late-Georgian merchant's house overlooking the river and Whitcliffe, has ten beds and is probably the best restaurant in town. When it opened the chef was from Inigo Jones in London and his assistant from Menage a Trois in New York. The Ludlow I remember was a town of butcher's sausage and black pudding, runner beans and sprouts, and, if it were Christmas, sherry trifle.

Oh come you on a Monday
When Ludlow Market hums
And Ludlow Bells are playing
"The Conquering Hero comes".

The ashes of A.E. Housman are interred in the churchyard of St Lawrence's, the largest parish church in Shropshire. The members of the Housman Society, a small body of the faithful, hold a meeting in Ludlow in the Spring; lunch (at the Bull, when I attended), a ceremony in the Church, a recital of his work in the churchyard, and then high tea back at the Bull. The Mayor and members of the society march solemnly in procession. Lulow loves its poet.

Market Day is still on Monday, and the fair, about which the poet sang, is still held on the First of May. Save perhaps for the most devoted admirers of Housman, Ludlow Fair is best avoided. The town is turned into a bedlam of steam whistles, canned music and candy floss, with Shropshire Lads taking on board pints of Ludlow ale which they later attempt, unsuccessfully, to carry home. The reality of fairs and fairgrounds is tat. Better by far to curl up in front of the fire on any other day of the year, and read all about it.

A few years ago, the Victorian Market Hall fell down. This was widely taken to be an Act of God, as the New Renaissance building (1887) was considered to be the only ugly building of any importance in the town. The local Civic Society began a lively debate as to what, if anything, should take its place in the szquare outside the castle. Its predecessor had been built in black and white by John Abel, the King's Carpenter, in the 17th century, and a similar work of his survives at Leominster and another at Ledbury in Herefordshire. Some thought a replica, suitably adapted, should be built; others argued that Ludlow's square, which was designed originally as an open space, but which had been in-filled over the years, should stay open, and, at the time of writing, the Monday market has reassembled under canvas.

The castle is a large and well-preserved ruin from which the Marches of Wales were governed in the years before 1536. It was whole until the roof lead was removed in the 18th century, and there are some who would persuade the Earl of Powys to restore some of the later buildings (Milton's Comus was first performed in the great hall), but so far without success. Edward V was proclaimed king in Ludlow, the princes in the tower left Ludlow for London where they were smothered, and the castle was the last fortress to hold out for the king in the Civil War. The chapel, which stands within the inner bailey, has a circular nave, one of two in England.

The castle, which is built of limestone (St Lawrence is built of red sandstone), overlooks the confluence of the rivers Teme and Corve, and stands upon a crag. It is haunted. Marion de Bruyere was in the habit of permitting her lover to visit her secretly in the castle at night. In the end he came armed with a hundred men who took the castle; Marion killed him with his own sword and then leapt to her death from the battlements of the Hanging Tower. The more bibulous Salopians claim to have seen her 12th-century ghost wandering about the castle.

Ludlow's pride is Broad Street which runs down from the 18th-century Butter Cross (1743) to the river. The Broad Gate spans the road, the last of the town's gates. It has a house on top.

The top of the street has shops, housed in handsome black and white, while, further down the hill, the street is lined with splendid Georgian mansions, the best of which is the Speaker's House. In the 1970s, the Speaker's House was on the market for less than £19,000 and needed central heating put in. In the 'nineties, the houses have all been fully restored, and are beyond the pockets of all save those who have done well out of the "big bang". The street runs north/south, and the handsome, walled gardens catch the sun. One garden has 78 varieties of clematis purchased, in the main, from Treasures of Tenbury Wells who specialise in the shrub.

To get the view that appears on a thousand posters and postcards of the town, you drive up to the Bowling Green pub on Whitcliffe, the wooded hill which rises to the west of Ludlow. Ludlow, castle and church, lies at one's feet, and the horizon is blocked off by the Titterstone and Brown Clee hills. It is as handsome a view as in all England.

A.E. Housman was an exquisite, if minor, poet. He saw his Shropshire as a solvent for his perplexities, but was intelligent enough to comprehend the illusions of total identification with nature. In the last verse of what I think is his finest poem, he wrote,

For nature, heartless, witless nature,
Will neither care nor know
What stranger's feet may find the meadow
And trespass there and go,
Nor ask amid the dews of morning
If they are mine or no

In 1936, Housman came back to Ludlow to be buried. A cherry tree – "Loveliest of trees, the cherry now" – is planted to mark his grave.

INDUSTRIAL RELICS, TITTERSTONE CLEE HILL

MEADOWS ABOVE TENBURY

SPRINGTIME NEAR BURWARTON

FARM-STEADING NEAR BRIDGENORTH

AUTUMN IN HOPE DALE

STANTON LACY CHURCHYARD

TITTERSTONE CLEE HILL

SUN-UP IN CORVE DALE

OIL-SEED RAPE AT DITTON PRIORS

HEATH CHAPEL, CLEE ST MARGARET

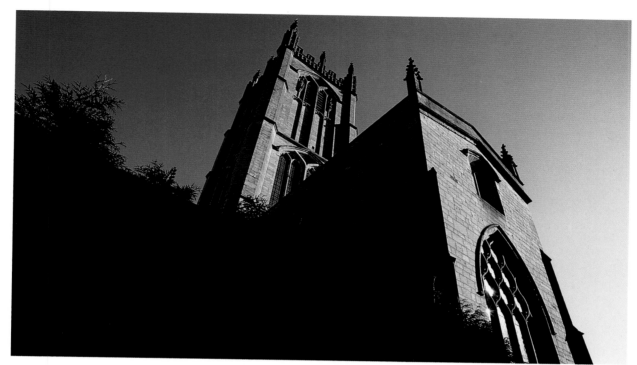

LUDLOW PARISH CHURCH

COLLEGE STREET, LUDLOW

THE GATEHOUSE, STOKESAY CASTLE

THE BULLRING, LUDLOW

WINTER SKY AT HEATH CHAPEL

KILVERT COUNTRY:
HEREFORDSHIRE

WOODS AT MORTIMER'S CROSS

CHAPTER 5

Burrington is a silent place. The village school has become a private house, there is a pretty black and white farm, two or three cottages, and a handsome church with an almost empty churchyard. Burrington lies in the Vale of Wigmore, the bed of an ice-age lake which in recent geological time overflowed, and by so doing allowed the Teme to cut the gorge through Bringewood Chase on its way to Ludlow and the Severn at Worcester. The river Teme must once have flowed past Amestrey into the plain of Hereford, but ice blocked its path. In consequence, the river now flows north-east, through the hills behind Burrington between 300ft-high cliffs. The Vale is flat and well farmed, and the river meanders across it, uncertain as to what direction it should take. The Vale is a basin surrounded by hills, which are themselves an extension of the Wenlock Edge. The result is a charming backwater, cut off from the outside world, invaded only by low-flying military jet aircraft. Climb the lane behind Burrington (it is unfit for motor cars) and a splendid view unfolds.

In the 'eighties, I spent the early part of August staying at Burrington. Church Bank is owned by Rosemary and Alan Laurie. It is the very best kind of "B&B", where four course dinners are cooked by Mrs. Laurie while her husband, a former housemaster at Shrewsbury School, serves at table. Had Rosemary Laurie cooked for me when I was at Shrewsbury, I might have been persuaded to stay on as an assistant master. The cottage is comfortable and full of books. The silence of the village is broken twice a day by the arrival of the Post Office van, the churchyard contains cast iron tomb "stones" mainly commemorating the Knight family, ironmasters of Downton Castle, and the river Teme meanders close to the front door. Peace, perfect peace with loved ones far away.

Wigmore is Mortimer territory, and Mortimer Forest covers much of the surrounding hills. Wigmore itself lies to the west on the road between Leintwardine and Mortimer's Cross, the site of a 13th century battle. The abbey has vanished, but the ruins of the castle remain, and the field which sweeps down from the keep to the road immediately north of the village was the scene of mediaeval tournaments attended by the Plantagenet kings. Edward V was a Mortimer, and the country a stronghold of the White Rose. Their ancient power is reflected in the west end of London by adjacent Mortimer and Wigmore streets.

Croft Castle, close to Mortimer's Cross, the scene of the Yorkist victory in the Wars of the Roses, is open to the public. In one of the public rooms there are two busts by John and Richard Riley of Prince Leopold and Princess Charlotte, the daughter of the Prince Regent. The busts are among the finest made in Staffordshire (£6,000 was asked recently for another of Princess Charlotte − the pair would fetch £15,000). What is so striking is the provenance of the pair at Croft. The Princess died in childbirth in 1816 and the nation mourned. Her physician was Sir Henry Croft, the then owner of the castle.

Near Croft is Lucton Church, which I nearly bought from an American electronics engineer. He had purchased the building from the Church Commissioners and had converted it into a charming house. The nave was the drawing room, the altar his kitchen. An upstairs floor had been added with views over the village and beyond. The chancel had been skilfully altered into a lobby and guest bedroom. Most spectacular of all, the tower had been glassed in at its top, and turned into the great man's study. Outside, the gravestones had been lifted and made to line the circumference of the circular churchyard like so many finger biscuits around a cake. The building had been tastefully and expensively adapted. It had a certain chic. I took out my cheque book and unscrewed my pen. But I could not persuade my wife to agree to the purchase. She said she felt she was not fit to live in a church. If it comes to that, who is?

In the past I could always tell when driving out of Shropshire into Hereford. The Hereford County Council, in the years long before its shot-gun marriage with Worcester, insisted that the hedges at crossroads were cut down and replaced by metal fencing in order to give the motorist warning of oncoming cars. How very sensible of the County Council. Herefordshire looks very different from Shropshire. There are even fewer people but they give the impression of living on a fatter land. The villages are of black and white - in Shropshire they are more often made of stone - and the Hereford country with its wooded cornstone hills is rich in orchards and hop fields.

In the 'eighties, the vineyards were replanted, and the county of "secret cider drinkers" (as it was described by a former Bishop of Hereford in an indignant letter to The Times) has taken enthusiastically to the local wines. They are white and a touch tart to the tongue.

If in Shropshire the Welsh hills have invaded the English plain, in Hereford the view to the west is blocked by the line of the Black Mountains with the great shelf of Hay's Bluff behind Hay-on-Wye providing a backdrop to the most pastoral of English counties. The soil is blood red and the woods deciduous. It is only in the Clun and Mortimer Forests, and on parts of the Longmynd, that the Forestry Commission has put its long lines of conifers on parade, turning England into Scandinavia.

Herefordshire is a red land where the hills are cultivated to their summits. It is prosperous, but not densely populated. The Saxon drove out the Celt and for more than a thousand years the dispossessed have gazed down enviously upon the lush lands of Hereford from the distant line of the Welsh mountains. The Normans ruled both and have left a legacy of ruined castles and keeps. Many of the Welsh have returned not with the sword but by stealth, and the Welsh influence, especially in the south of Herefordshire is still strong. Hereford is, to my mind, a disappointing city, not as fine as Shrewsbury, although it can boast an Anglican cathedral and a famous map of the world. It also has Bulmer's Cider works, and, on a railway siding nearby, the King George V, once the "flagship" of the old Great Western Railway. Twice a year the locomotive comes to life, and steams between Shrewsbury and Hereford with a train of Pullman coaches. It is greeted everywhere as an old friend.

The great day of the train was the time when ordinary folk had to do most of their travelling on foot. Only the rich rode horses. One famous walker was Francis Kilvert. Kilvert is the third writer who has chosen to write about the Welsh border country. Mary Webb wrote about the Shropshire Lakes and the Stiperstones in *Precious Bane* and *Gone to Earth,* A.E. Housman wrote *A Shropshire Lad.* Francis Kilvert, the Curate of Clyro on the borders of what was Radnorshire (now Powys) and Hereford and Worcester, wrote about the southern marches. Thus a romantic novelist, a poet and a diarist have combined to sing the praises of the Borderland. They were a mixed bag. Mary Webb suffered from hot, literary, flushes (she died of Bright's disease, one of the symptoms of which is a heightened imagination). Housman was described by a fellow don whom he had undoubtedly once offended as "descended from a long line of maiden aunts" and Kilvert was simply a marvellous "camera", a reporter who chronicled the every-day affairs of the borderland in the 1870s. Let me give you an extract from his diary:

1870, 9 June

In the night there came a cooler wind and fair showers out of the west. The falling white blossoms of the clematis drift in at the open window on the fresh morning breeze. In the garden there are red roses, and blue hills beyond. Last night the moon was shining in at my west window through the lacing bows of the mountain ash — the moonbeams fell across the bed and I saw "the gusty shadow sway" on the white bed curtain.

Kilvert described what he saw, not the effect it produced on him, and his diaries — only a small proportion of what he wrote remains — give a vivid picture of what England must have been like in that most fascinating of times, the day before yesterday. He has become a cult figure. Just as the Housman Society comes once a year to Ludlow to celebrate the poet, so the Kilvert Society visits Clyro, Clifford and Hay on Wye to retrace the footsteps of the master. That is no mean task, given the amount of ground Kilvert seems to have covered.

In 1870 he was 29, and the son of a Wiltshire parson whose family originated in Shropshire. He died nine years later at Bredwardine, of peritonitis, two years after his marriage. It was the age before antibiotics. His diaries only came to light in the late 'thirties. Kilvert came to Clyro when the countryside was precisely at the peak of its beauty. The village communities were still intact, the country was not empty, which it is today, save perhaps in summer when the tourists come. There was no traffic on the unmetalled roads. The fields were manicured, a landscape which was prosperous and brought to perfection by the work of generations. The diaries are a marvellous read. He writes of the clear days when, from the hills behind Clyro, the Clee Hills and even the Caradoc at Stretton, 40 miles away, were clearly visible.

FARM BUILDINGS NEAR KNIGHTON

CAST-IRON GRAVESTONE AT BURRINGTON

BLACK MOUNTAINS, ABOVE CUSOP

EARDISLAND

BLACKCURRANT VINES NEAR PRESTEIGNE

SUNSET OVER THE WYE VALLEY

BURIAL GROUND AT WIGMORE

EARDISLAND

BLACK MOUNTAIN PONIES

STUBBLE-FIELDS NEAR WALFORD

BREDWARDINE CHURCH

THE WYE VALLEY FROM CUSOP

HEREFORD CATHEDRAL

HEDGEROW OUTSIDE HAY-ON-WYE

SUMMERS ON THE LONGMYND

THE LONGMYND

EPILOGUE

In 1991 my aunt Daisy, who had left Shropshire for New Zealand in the early 'twenties, died in Auckland at the age of 94. Like so many old people nowadays she took the precaution of recording some hours of reminiscence on audio cassette, bequeathing to her relatives a picture of an England which has long since vanished.

I met my aunt only once, when she visited this country in 1972. She was then in her seventies, and had the ruddy complexion of a countrywoman and the stamina of an American tourist. She had been born at the turn of the century at Wistanstow, and once we had shown her the sights of London she departed post-haste for Shropshire to re-discover lost relatives and a distant past.

In her tapes she brings the dead to life. She was my mother's elder sister, the fourth child of my railwayman grandfather. She was born in the rented stone cottage, under Wenlock Edge, which is the focus of my childhood memories. Rectory Cottage was the property of the local parson; later, it passed into the hands of the Grove estate, home of the Greenes. Mr Greene was Tory MP for Shrewsbury, his wife the heir to a chamber-pot fortune.

The Grove, which I can just remember as a dismally ugly late-Victorian house, was pulled down in the 'fifties to make way for a broiler-chicken factory. As great houses go, the Grove came late and went early.

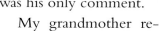

WISTANSTOW PARISH CHURCH

On my desk is a sepia photograph of my grandmother taken in 1902. She was then in her late thirties and had just been widowed. She is seated at the cottage door. Her six children surround her, the youngest a babe in arms, the eldest, Campbell, a boy aged 12, wearing his suit and a mourning band. It is like an illustration from a novel by Thomas Hardy.

My grandfather had been killed by a rogue engine on the line at Leominster; his moustache, as family legend has it, was later found half a mile down the line. News of an accident reached the cottage "up the Common" and my grandmother set off to walk the three miles to Craven Arms, with babe in arms; she had gone barely a step before running into her father, a farm labourer in his seventies who lived with the family, coming up the lane. "No use you'm going there – he's dead," was his only comment.

My grandmother re-ceived a certain amount of compensation from the railway, but was kept alive by the Greenes, who employed her sons in turn as gardeners or game-keepers and arranged for her to kennel their dogs. A friendly farmer had long permitted the family to plant two rows of potatoes around the edge of one of his fields a mile or so away at Felhampton. She bought a mangle and took to washing the surplices from the village church. Squire and parish then stood proxy for what today would have been the responsibility of the social services, as must have often happened in the last century.

Such distant memories contain both light and shade. Breakfast before attending the village school was usually "dukes", a word I had never come across until I listened to Aunt Daisy's cassette. Dukes is bread broken up in sweet, milky tea. For other meals, eggs were halved, but there was always bacon, a tribute to the cottage pig. Beer was home-brewed from mangels, and wine made from elder-berries. Treats consisted of giant suet puddings with a crust which was anointed with butter and sugar. Summers are remembered by my aunt with affection, but the winters must have been vile; frozen children, cold school rooms, and, in all probability, inadequate clothing. But there was a big fire in the cottage, and slices of toast and beef dripping. The Great War took the three boys to France; the only jobs for the girls at the time were going into service, teaching or nursing.

WENLOCK EDGE FROM TICKLERTON

well in the garden, a wash house from which my auntie May would emerge in a cloud of Monday steam, and a two-seater lavatory at the bottom of the garden. The scullery contained a large jar of pickled onions, the kitchen had a black-leaded grate, a cottage picture of a small girl winningly presenting a bouquet of flowers within a maple frame, which I have acquired, and a grandfather clock which, by being kept twenty minutes fast, aped the clocks of King George V at Sandringham. There was a small parlour, largely unused. The stairs were guarded by a door, and the three upstairs bedrooms were connected the one to another. The beds were of feathers, and the upstairs windows, small. In the summer, and the summers of the late 'thirties were hot, the front door was kept open and the windows smelt of geraniums and wasps.

Aunt Daisy gave a harrowing account of my grand-mother's death from cancer. She took two years to die, being nursed constantly by my aunt, who would hold her mother's leg in a comfortable position (the growth was pressing on the sciatic nerve) until she fell asleep. I wonder how much easier her death would have been made today? My aunt's legacy – she was the last of her immediate family to die – has been to open windows long shut, and, by so doing, to revive ancient memories. Sadly, she, too, died of her mother's complaint, although, I am told, swiftly and painlessly. How much better most things became in the course of her long lifetime.

When I was young in the late 'thirties, my family still went whinberrying on the Longmynd, although prosperity had removed the need to make pocket money, as had once been the case. We would picnic in some style up Ashes Valley (cold ham and farm cider), having arrived in a Morris 8. The whinberries, such as we bothered to pick, were turned later into pies.

The cottage, even as I remember it before the war, must have been typical of Shropshire. Built of limestone with a slate roof, it had once been two, but my grandmother had made it into one. Oil lamps – electricity did not arrive until well after the war, a

OCTOBER FROST IN WISTANSTOW

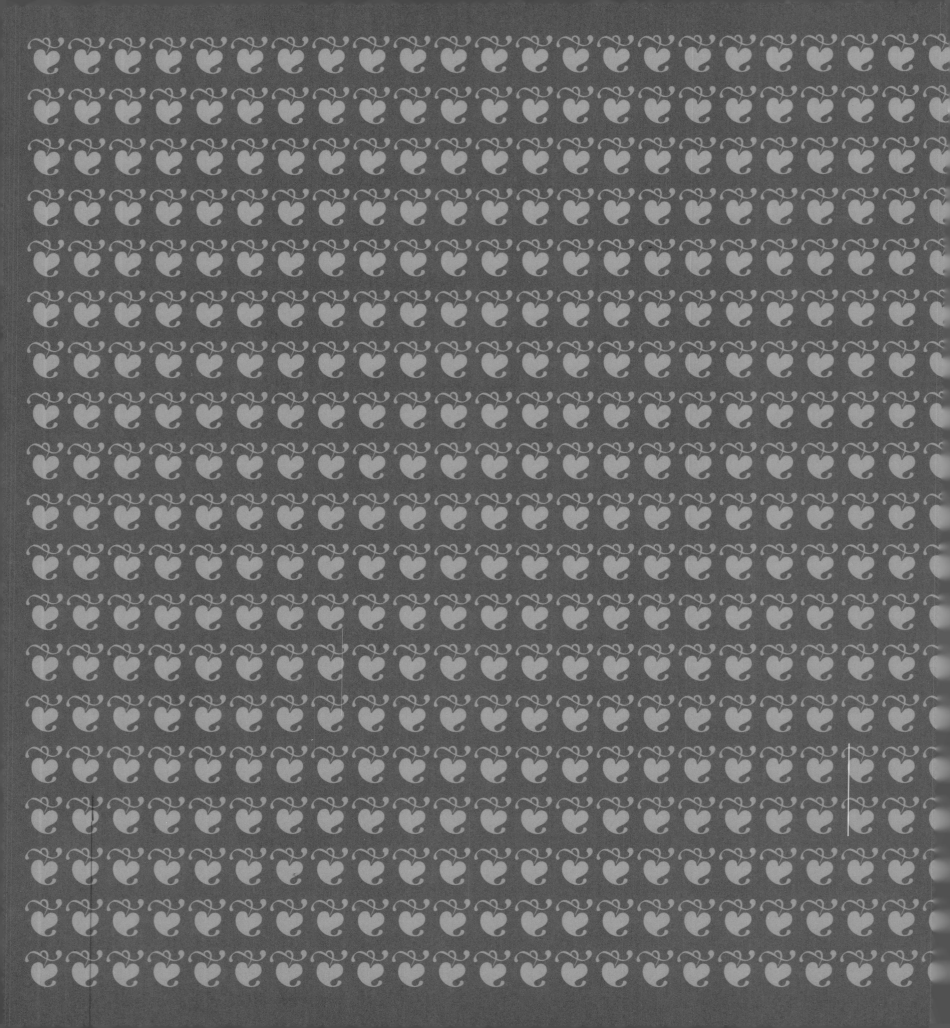